DOOMED HISTORY

MT. VESUVIUS ERUPTS!

Pompeii, 79 CE

T0025521

by Nancy Dickman

BEARPORT
PUBLISHING

Minneapolis, Minnesota

Bearport Publishing Company Product Development Team
President: Jen Jenson; Director of Product Development: Spencer Brinker; Senior Editor: Allison Juda; Editor: Charly Haley; Associate Editor: Naomi Reich; Senior Designer: Colin O'Dea; Associate Designer: Elena Klinkner; Product Development Assistant: Anita Stasson

Brown Bear Books
Children's Publisher: Anne O'Daly; Design Manager: Keith Davis;
Picture Manager: Sophie Mortimer

Library of Congress Cataloging-in-Publication Data is available at www.loc.gov or upon request from the publisher.

ISBN: 979-8-88509-083-4 (hardcover)
ISBN: 979-8-88509-090-2 (paperback)
ISBN: 979-8-88509-097-1 (ebook)

For more information, write to Bearport Publishing, 5357 Penn Avenue South, Minneapolis, MN 55419. Printed in the United States of America.

CONTENTS

IN THE SHADOW OF VESUVIUS

It was a beautiful summer morning in southern Italy. But in just 24 hours, the area would be almost completely destroyed.

The Bay of Naples sits just over 100 miles (160 km) south of Rome. Hundreds of years ago, towns and cities dotted its shoreline, with many well-off Romans setting up vacation homes there. Pompeii was one of the largest cities on the bay, nestled between the smaller towns Stabiae and Herculaneum. At the northwestern end of the bay was Misenum, which the Roman navy used as a base. A mountain called Vesuvius towered over it all.

Life in Pompeii

Pompeii was similar to many other Roman cities. There were public baths and an arena where people could watch **gladiator** fights. Pompeii had shops, theaters, and even fast-food cafes called *thermopolia*. August 24 was a day just like any other. People were shopping in the markets and sharing the news of the day at the baths. But by the next sunrise, many of these people would be dead.

Mt. Vesuvius rises more than 4,000 feet (1,220 m) above sea level.

THE FIRST SIGNS OF TROUBLE

Four days earlier, people living in Pompeii and the surrounding towns had been shaken by a small earthquake.

Earthquakes were very common in this area, so no one paid them much attention. In fact, the citizens were still repairing buildings damaged in a severe quake 17 years earlier. Earthquakes were considered worth putting up with in order to live in this beautiful area with its rich soil. The crops grown here had made many of Pompeii's citizens wealthy.

Volcanic ash from previous eruptions made the soil perfect for growing grapes.

A Deadly Secret

Small earthquakes continued for several days, with the people of Pompeii living life as usual. At the time, no one knew Vesuvius was hiding a deadly secret—the mountain was actually a volcano! It hadn't erupted for hundreds of years, but the earthquakes were a sign that it was getting ready to blow again.

A Famous Scientist

One of the citizens going about his everyday life was Caius Plinius Secundus, also known as Pliny the Elder. He was an officer in the Roman navy and a well-known writer who studied the natural world. On the morning of August 24, he was at his home in Misenum with his sister and her 17-year-old son, known as Pliny the Younger.

Pliny the Elder's encyclopedia, *Natural History*, contained information about Earth, plants, animals, stars, and more.

The Mountain Wakes Up

At about noon, Pliny's sister pointed to a cloud pouring out from Vesuvius. From nearly 20 miles (32 km) away they couldn't tell exactly what was happening. But while they gazed at the smoke, a messenger arrived from Pliny's friend begging to be rescued from her home near the foot of the volcano. Realizing that the cloud must mean danger, Pliny the Elder ordered warships to set out to save anybody they could.

Pliny the Younger compared the shape of the cloud to the umbrella pine trees that grew in the area.

IN PLINY'S WORDS

The only eyewitness account of the eruption comes from Pliny the Younger. He wrote, "My mother pointed out a cloud with an odd size and appearance that had just formed. . . . Like a true scholar, my uncle saw at once that it deserved closer study and ordered a boat to be prepared."

DISASTER STRIKES

Misenum was miles from the volcano. In towns closer to Vesuvius, things were already becoming dangerous.

By the time Pliny the Elder's ships launched, hot ash had already started to rain down on the areas closer to the volcano. It settled on roofs and streets, rapidly piling up into a thick layer. Each hour, it got about 6 inches (15 cm) deeper.

Volcanic ash quickly covers everything near an eruption.

Wind direction

ITALY

Naples

Herculaneum

Misenum

▲ Vesuvius

Ash cloud

Pompeii

Stabiae

N
W — E
S

Wind blew the ash cloud away from Misenum, but straight toward Pompeii.

Panic!

Soon, a cloud of thick ash was blocking out much of the sunlight. The hot ash stank like rotten eggs because of the **sulfur** gas spewing out from the volcano. People hadn't known that Vesuvius was a volcano, and they didn't know what would happen next. Some decided to flee, taking whatever they could carry with them. Others decided to wait it out, hoping things would get better.

Falling Rocks

It wasn't just ash that was raining from the sky. Small lumps of volcanic rock called **pumice** were falling, too. Although pumice is light and full of holes, the volcano also released heavier, fist-size rocks that had been torn loose from the walls of the volcano by the force of the eruption. The fallen ash and stone began to pile up. By 5:00 p.m., roofs in Pompeii were collapsing under its weight, trapping or killing those still inside.

Pumice is so light that it floats in water.

PUMICE

Pumice forms during a violent eruption. Thick, sticky **lava** has gas bubbles trapped inside. When it flies out of the volcano, it cools to form rock. The bubbles leave holes behind.

Pompeii's streets would have been filled with terrified men, women, and children.

The Rush to Escape

The roads were soon clogged with people running for their lives. Some of them tied pillows to their heads as protection from falling rocks. Out on the water, Pliny's boat was also showered with hot ash and pumice, but he continued on to the city of Stabiae, which wasn't badly affected yet.

Waiting for Rescue

For many nearby cities, the rain of ash and stone continued late into the night. But the coastal town Herculaneum had been mostly spared so far. The wind had carried most of the ash elsewhere, giving many of its people the chance to **evacuate**. Some of those who remained took shelter near the shore. But shortly after 11:00 p.m., the eruption of Vesuvius reached a new, deadlier stage.

Herculaneum had many rich residents who were very proud of their beautifully decorated homes.

A pyroclastic surge is so hot and moves so quickly that there is often no time to escape.

A Wave of Heat

The ash cloud coming out of Vesuvius had reached a height of about 20 miles (32 km) when it suddenly collapsed. A pyroclastic surge came crashing down the mountain, its mix of extremely hot gases, molten rock, pumice, and ash speeding out from the mountain at up to 200 miles per hour (320 kph). Anyone left in Herculaneum would have been killed instantly when the surge hit, as it raised temperatures to over 400 degrees Fahrenheit (204 degrees Celsius).

LIFE OR DEATH

Herculaneum had disappeared, buried under ash and lava. But there was more to come—Pompeii would be next.

The collapsing ash cloud sent out more pyroclastic surges, and this time they were headed straight for Pompeii. At 6:30 a.m. one of these surges hit the massive city. Historians don't know how many of Pompeii's 12,000 residents were still there at the time, but they are certain that none of them would have survived.

Killed by Heat

Scientists estimate the pyroclastic surge that crashed into Pompeii had a temperature of at least 480°F (249°C). That would have been hot enough to melt any silverware in the kitchens of Pompeii. Even rooms away from doors and windows, where some people sheltered, would have reached a temperature hotter than boiling water. People died instantly, **suffocated** by the heat. Their bodies were quickly buried under collapsing buildings and a deep layer of ash and pumice.

Most buildings in Pompeii had roofs of clay tiles. By the time of the surge, ash and pumice had buried the first stories completely.

Safety in Stabiae?

Meanwhile, Pliny the Elder had spent the night safely in Stabiae. He was at a **villa** owned by his friend Pomponianus. Pliny took a bath and managed to get some sleep while most of the rest of the household stayed awake, terrified. The pyroclastic surges that destroyed Herculaneum and Pompeii missed Stabiae, though ash and pumice were still burying the city.

Like many Roman homes, Pomponianus's villa was built around a central courtyard.

Pliny's ship was a small, fast boat powered by three dozen rowers.

End of the Line

When the sun rose the next day, its light could not break through the heavy ash cloud that hung over the city. People needed torches to see. Pliny went down to the shore to see if they could launch a boat, but the waves were too high. Pliny the Elder began to feel unwell, and before he could take a drink from the water he asked for, he collapsed and died. Modern historians believe he probably suffocated on the sulfur in the air.

Everyone escaping Misenum had to crowd onto the same narrow strip of land.

Race to Escape

Pliny's sister and his nephew, Pliny the Younger, were still back at home in Misenum. The deadly surges had missed them, but the ground shook so badly overnight that they couldn't sleep. In the morning, they decided to join the crowds fleeing the town. So much ash was falling that they often had to stop to shake it off.

IN PLINY'S WORDS

This is how Pliny the Younger described their journey. "We could hear women shrieking, children crying, and men shouting. Some were calling for their parents, their children, or their wives. . . . Some people were so frightened of dying that they actually prayed for death. Many begged for the help of the gods, but even more imagined that there were no gods left and that the last eternal night had fallen on the world. . . . I was only kept going by the consolation that the whole world was **perishing** with me."

Pliny the Younger later wrote about his escape in a letter to his friend Tacitus.

A Desperate Dash

As they struggled along the crowded road, Pliny the Younger and his mother looked out to the coast. They saw the waters of the sea pulled away from shore, leaving fish and other sea creatures stranded. This was a warning sign of a **tsunami**. Huge waves could come crashing to shore any moment. Luckily, Pliny the Younger and his mother had escaped, and it appeared that the eruption was finally slowing.

Tsunamis can leave a wide path of destruction in their wake.

Ashfall after a volcano can range from a few inches to many feet deep.

The Last Blows

That morning, three more pyroclastic surges hit Pompeii. These were even hotter than the ones before. Scientists estimate that the fourth surge reached 572°F (300°C). All the people in Pompeii were already dead, but the surges dumped at least another 9 ft. (2.7 m) of ash and stone on the city. When the haze finally cleared, the whole region was unrecognizable.

WHAT HAPPENED NEXT

The eruption was finally over. But Pompeii, Herculaneum, and several other towns were gone.

No one knows how many people died in the eruption. About 1,500 bodies have been found in Pompeii and Herculaneum so far, but it's thought that as many as 16,000 may have died. Those who escaped were left with nothing. Their cities were completely buried. Herculaneum was hidden under 75 ft. (23 m) of volcanic **debris**.

TOMB ROBBERS

Pompeii was not buried in debris as deeply as Herculaneum. In the years after the eruption, some people dug down into the ash to steal valuables. They stole some of the marble statues from the Forum, Pompeii's main square.

Refugees

Survivors from the eruption became **refugees**. Many of them settled in Naples as well as other towns and cities north of the volcano. The Roman **emperor**, Titus, raised money to help these people who no longer had homes.

The Forum was the main meeting place for the people of Pompeii. It was surrounded by temples and public buildings.

Rediscovery

Pompeii and Herculaneum lay buried until the 1700s. Then, people began to **excavate** the ruins. They were amazed at what they found. The remains were like a time capsules of ancient Roman life. Many buildings were still standing, and art such as paintings and **mosaics** survived in good condition. Archaeologists even found **graffiti** scrawled on walls and bakeries with loaves still in the ovens.

Their Final Moments

People who died in the pyroclastic surges had been immediately covered in ash. When the ash cooled and hardened, it created a kind of shell over the bodies. Over time, the flesh rotted away, leaving body-shaped hollows within the ash casing. Scientist filled these hollows with plaster to make models of the victims in the moment of their deaths. The casts bring life to the horror of Mt. Vesuvius's eruption.

Many of the casts of Pompeii's victims are on display at the site.

Tourists can walk through a theater where Pompeii's residents once watched plays.

A Trip Back in Time

Archaeologists are still excavating the buried cities, but a lot of what has been uncovered is open to tourists. Walking the streets is like taking a trip back in time. Visitors can wander through the houses, shops, and squares, seeing what life was like in Roman times. In the distance, Vesuvius still towers over the region. Brave tourists can even hike up a steep path to see its steaming **crater**!

Another Eruption?

Vesuvius has erupted many times since the destruction of Pompeii. There was another bad explosion in 1631 that killed several thousands of people. Vesuvius's most recent eruption was in 1944, but another could come some day soon. Today, there are many more people living in the danger zone than during Roman times, so scientists watch the volcano carefully. If they see warning signs, they can order an evacuation. No one wants to see another disaster like Pompeii.

An eruption today could affect up to three million people living in the area.

KEY DATES

79 CE

August 20 The first of a series of small earthquakes hits the area around Pompeii

August 24

About noon People in Misenum see a large cloud over Vesuvius

1:00 p.m. Ash and pumice begin to fall on Pompeii

5:00 p.m. Buildings in Pompeii begin to collapse

6:45 p.m. Pliny's boat lands at Stabiae

August 25

1:00 a.m. The ash cloud collapses, and the first pyroclastic surge hits Herculaneum

6:30 a.m. A pyroclastic surge hits Pompeii, killing everyone left in the town

6:45 a.m. Pliny the Elder dies at Stabiae

8:00 a.m. A final surge hits Pompeii, burying it

1709 Workmen discover the buried ruins of Herculaneum

1738 Archaeologists start to excavate the ruins of Herculaneum

1748 Archaeologists begin to excavate the remains of Pompeii

1863 The first casts are made of the bodies of Pompeii's victims

1944 The most recent eruption of Vesuvius

QUIZ How much have you learned about Pompeii? It's time to test your knowledge! Then, check the answers on page 32.

1. **Which mountain towers over Pompeii?**
   a. Etna
   b. Vesuvius
   c. Stromboli

2. **What was the first sign that an eruption might happen?**
   a. earthquakes
   b. a tsunami
   c. strong winds

3. **How did Pliny the Elder try to rescue people?**
   a. in a horse-drawn carriage
   b. by building a shelter
   c. by boat

4. **What is pumice?**
   a. a kind of light rock formed during an eruption
   b. the remains of a body buried in ash
   c. a type of Roman vehicle

5. **Which town was buried even deeper than Pompeii?**
   a. Misenum
   b. Herculaneum
   c. Stabiae